Turn Your Story Into Cash
Writing & Launching Your Book

Author: Judi Moreo

Las Vegas, Nevada 89120
United States of America

Copyright 2019 by Turning Point International
All rights reserved

No portion of this book may be reproduced in any form or by any means without permission in writing from the publisher, except for the inclusion of brief quotations in a review.

Cover design and typesetting: Jake Naylor

ISBN: 978-0-9882307-4-3
Library of Congress Control Number: 2019911564

3315 E. Russell Road, Ste. A4-404
Las Vegas, Nevada 89105
(702) 283-4567

Published in the United States of America

Disclaimer

This book is designed to provide information on writing, publishing, marketing, promoting and distributing books. It is sold with the understanding that the publisher and author are not engaged in rendering legal, accounting or other professional services. If legal or other expert assistance is required, the services of a competent professional should be sought.

It is not the purpose of this book to reprint all the information that is otherwise available to authors and/or publishers, but instead to complement, amplify and supplement other texts.

You are urged to read all the available material, learn as much as possible about self-publishing, and tailor the information to your individual needs.

Self-publishing is not a get-rich-quick scheme. Anyone who decides to write and publish a book must expect to invest a lot of time and effort into it. For many people, self-publishing is more lucrative than selling manuscripts to another publisher, and many have built solid, growing, rewarding businesses.

Every effort has been made to make this book as complete and as accurate as possible. However, *there may be mistakes*, both typographical and in content. Therefore, this text should be used only as a general guide and not as the ultimate source of writing and publishing information. Furthermore, this book contains information on writing and publishing that is current only up to the printing date.

The purpose of this book is to educate and entertain. The author and Turning Point International shall have neither liability nor responsibility to any person or entity with respect to any loss or damage caused, or alleged to have been caused, directly or indirectly, by the information contained in this book.

If you do not wish to be bound by the above, you may return this book to the publisher with your receipt for a full refund.

About the Author
Judi Moreo, CSP

Successful entrepreneur, author, motivator, podcaster, and television show host, Judi Moreo is the author of eleven books including two international best sellers, *"You Are More Than Enough"* and *"Ignite the Spark."* Publisher of both the *Life Choices* book series and *Choices* Magazine, Judi is the host of the popular *Choices* with Judi Moreo internet radio show and the *World of Creativity* television show,

Judi Moreo is one of the most admired personal growth trainers and coaches in the world. Judi has earned the prestigious Certified Speaking Professional designation from the National Speakers Association. Less than 12% of the speakers in the world hold this certification. Judi has informed, inspired, challenged, motivated, and entertained audiences in twenty-nine countries around the globe with her unique speaking style. She is often hired as a coach/mentor by writers, speakers, entrepreneurs, and corporate executives who want to develop and market their skills.

If your desire is to have more success, write better books, give better speeches, and get more recognition, let Judi Moreo help you make that happen.

Contact:
(702) 283-4567
judi@ judimoreo.com

Skype:
crystal hill 21

Table of Contents

Section 1: Planning Your Book and Launch — 1

- Determine the Purpose of Your Book — 1
- Who Are You Writing For? — 3
- Marketing Research — 4
- Creating A Writing Schedule — 5
- Resources to Help You Write Faster — 7
- What Will You Outsource — 8
- Marketing Your Book — 9
- Launch Day Tips and Tactics — 10
- Checklist — 12
- Worksheet — 16

Section 2: Writing Your Book — 18

- Create an Outline — 18
- Flesh Out Each Chapter — 19
- Three Common Obstacles That Sideline Writers — 21
- How to Get Your Book Done Quickly — 22
- Keeping Your Writing Sessions Productive — 24
- Using Accountability to Get Your Book Done — 25
- Capturing the Elusive Beginning — 27
- Mastering the Ending of Your Book — 28
- Checklist — 30
- Worksheet — 33

Section 3: Publishing Your Book — 36

- Why Self-Publishing is Awesome — 36
- Who to Hire When You Self-Publish — 38
- How to Self-Publish — 39

Digital Downloads	41
Your Print On-Demand Options	42
Self-Publishing Mistakes to Avoid	43
Promoting Your Book Before the Release	45
Celebrating Release Day	47
Checklist	49
Worksheet	52

Section 4: Marketing Your Book — 56

Advertise Your Book on Social Media	56
How to Advertise Your Book on Reading Websites	58
Using Giveaways to Promote Your Book	59
Polishing Your Author Page	61
Creating and Building Your Email List	62
Interacting in Groups and Forums	63
Position Yourself as an Expert	65
Promoting Your Book Offline	66
Checklist	68
Worksheet	72

Section 1
Planning Your Book and Launch

When it comes to creating and launching your book, it may be tempting to just dive into the world of writing and publishing. But this can leave you feeling scattered, uncertain of your message, and overwhelmed by your to-do list.

Fortunately, planning is the answer. When you have a plan in place for how you'll write and launch your book, the process is much more enjoyable. Here's how to get started with your very own plan:

Determine the Purpose of Your Book

Before writing a single word, you want to get clear on why you're writing your book. When you know what you want, it's easier to make decisions about publishing. Here are a few common reasons why people publish a book:

Some online business owners publish books because they want to grow their platform. When you publish a book, thousands of people can discover your work. This can lead to public speaking opportunities, new client relationships, and even joint venture offers.

However, it's important to understand that your book needs to be related to your platform. For example, if you're a health and fitness coach and you publish a book about saving money, you're not likely to gain any traction.

Instead, stick to a topic that you can use to showcase your knowledge. A book about gardening with a 'grow your own healthy foods' slant would probably appeal to your community.

Turn Your Story Into Cash: Writing & Launching Your Book

Another reason you might want to publish a book is to establish your expertise and authority. When reporters and journalists look for sources to interview, they begin by looking for thought leaders in the industry. If you have a book published, it instantly makes you look like a knowledgeable professional.

Publishing a book also helps build your credibility. If you tackle a difficult topic in your book and present solutions that your audience can implement, then you'll be seen as a problem solver. If you leverage this talent, you could get paid work as a consultant.

There's a third reason you may choose to publish your book—for profit. If you're knowledgeable about your topic and you've found a unique viewpoint, then you can use your book to create another income stream. If you keep publishing books regularly, you can grow this stream until it's a raging river of revenue.

While you can absolutely make a living from simply publishing books, keep in mind that it can take some time to build an author brand. You'll need to spend time and money promoting your books as you grow your list of titles.

Some people want to publish a book to build up their confidence. When you've written a long book, it's easier to take on new challenges because you know you have what it takes to tackle big projects. This newfound confidence can attract potential clients who are eager to work with you.

Not only does publishing a book give you more confidence in your abilities, it also helps you solidify your brand. You know what your mission is, and this makes it easier to communicate your message with those around you.

Many authors find it's simpler to go after big opportunities after they've published a book. This is often due to embracing a new mindset. You're no longer plagued with intense self-doubt and overwhelmed with fear.

Instead, you'll look at new opportunities for what they really are—chances to grow and learn. With this mindset, it helps you put obstacles and setbacks into perspective. You'll also be more focused and have the ability to evaluate new ideas with a positive outlook.

Planning Your Book and Launch

Whatever your reason for writing and publishing a book, be honest about it. Embrace your ambition and take your message to the masses through the power of self-publishing!

Who Are You Writing for?

After you've established your goal for your book, you need to think about who your audience will be. This is one of the most important decisions you'll have to make. All of your other choices will flow from this one, so take some time to reflect before you pick. If you're having difficulty with this step, here are a few tips to get you thinking:

Start by identifying the topic you'll be writing about. This should be the topic that you can tie into your business. For example, if you want to be a highly sought after financial consultant, don't write a book about dentistry. People who read your book won't be interested in your financial services.

If you decide that you want to be an expert on animal care and training, your book audience would be pet parents. If you want to be an authority in art or design, your book audience would be artists and creatives.

As you're thinking about your audience, pause and do some keyword research. Keyword research will show you how often your term is searched for by web users every week or month.

Keep in mind that if you pick a topic that's rarely searched, then it may be a sign that the niche is too small. You may need to broaden your idea or pick a new niche.

If you pick a topic that's searched for frequently, then that's a sign you'll need to come up with a unique way to stand out. Otherwise, you'll be competing against millions of other books that cover the exact same information.

The easiest and most helpful way to begin your research is to use Google's Keyword Tool. It's a free tool, but you will need a Google account to sign in, if you don't already have one.

After you log in, select the option to find new keywords and get search volume data. Then, enter keywords that describe your book topic. For example, if you want to write a book about caring for an aging dog, do some research and see what terms are used to find information about this topic.

You might discover that the term 'senior dog' is searched for more often than 'aging dog'. This knowledge will make it easier to tailor your content to your readers.

Pay attention to how you feel during your keyword research. If you're getting more excited as you search, it's a sign you've picked an audience that you'll love to help. But, if you don't find yourself enjoying this step in the process, it might be time to reevaluate your target demographic.

Market Research: What Your Audience Expects

You know your niche and you know what audience you'll be serving. You may think you're finally ready to start writing. Before you begin, there's one vital step that you don't want to skip—doing your market research.

Market research will allow you to see what your community wants and expects from a book. Imagine spending hours writing and publishing your book, only to discover that no one's buying it. That would be very disappointing.

Fortunately, you can avoid this by focusing on your community from the very start of the writing and publishing process. Here's how to do your homework and learn what readers really want from your book:

You need to find comparable titles to yours. These will be books on the same subject matter. For example, if you plan to write about nutrition, you should search Amazon Books for nutrition. You may want to make a list of book titles and authors, so you can explore them again later on.

But for now, look over the results and think about your book. With so many books on one topic, your book needs to be unique so it will stand out. Try to look for gaps in the market, meaning reader needs that other authors have neglected to capitalize on.

You can also look through Amazon's Best Seller lists. These are the top 100 books in any given category. To find these books, go to your favorite search engine and type in "Amazon Best Sellers (Niche)" without quotations. Replace the word niche with your niche.

Doing this allows you to quickly and easily study different niches. If you see the same themes emerging again and again, write them down. These themes allow you to see what's popular with your community right now.

Planning Your Book and Launch

Next, examine the covers on the various books in your niche's best-sellers list. Look for what fonts and colors are used. Pay attention to what images are used for the covers.

Are they bright and colorful photos with script font? Are they muted colors with big fonts and an image of the author? If a particular cover appeals to you, make a note of it. When you're ready to hire a book designer later, you'll be glad you did.

Click on some of the books in your niche and read the reviews. Reviews are a gold mine for new authors because they allow you to see what your readers want and expect from niche books. For example, are reviewers complaining that new leadership book was too long?

Are they frustrated with that cookbook because it didn't include enough pictures? Do they find the personal finance book too analytical and boring? These are good notes to take that can help shape the book as you're working on it.

Don't forget to explore the price of the books in your niche. Some niches may charge more for their books because the information is specialized. For example, a book that's about a complicated computing language may sell for $14.99. A book on nutrition may only sell for $4.99. It depends on the niche and how much your target market is willing to pay for your information.

Creating a Writing Schedule You Can Stick With

It's easy to say you want to do something, like writing and publishing a book. But that's not enough. If you don't create a plan that details how you'll do it, then it won't get done. A writing schedule is a terrific action plan. It allows you to brainstorm specific goals and assign achievable deadlines to your project.

You can begin creating your schedule by evaluating how you're currently spending your time. It can be helpful to write out what a typical day looks like for you. Make sure to include both your personal and professional activities.

After you're done, review your typical day and look for pockets of time that you could dedicate to your book. If you're stretched thin and can't find any time to devote to your new goal, then look for tasks that you don't personally need to oversee. For example, cleaning your home doesn't have

Turn Your Story Into Cash: Writing & Launching Your Book

to be done by you. You could hire a company and outsource this task. That would give you an extra 1-3 hours of time to use for writing.

Outsourcing doesn't always work for everyone. If you don't have the money to outsource or you simply don't want the hassle, then consider delegating. Cleaning your home, preparing meals, and other tasks can be handled by a partner or older children and teens.

You can also look for areas in your day or week where you could make a temporary sacrifice. If you spend several hours binge-watching your favorite shows on Netflix, consider giving this up for a few weeks until you finish writing your book.

Thinking about writing a book can make you feel a bit overwhelmed. That's why you want to break it down into smaller tasks.

Many writers and entrepreneurs break their books down chapter by chapter. By focusing on one chapter at a time, you'll see that you will make more progress and be energized to work on your book regularly.

Before you sit down to write the chapter, take some time to brainstorm ideas and outline a few thoughts. This doesn't have to be a formal outline. It's fine to use a few bullet points to quickly jot down ideas you want to cover. When you have a quick outline in place, it cuts down on procrastination and allows you to come to your project ready to work.

If you're like most people, ideas for your book will pop into your head while you're driving, showering, or doing other activities. The perfect next paragraph will seem to leap into your mind, so use your phone to capture these moments of inspiration.

Try to keep any notes or memos you record saved in the same folder where you're storing your book. This will prevent you from spending hours searching for that one quote you wanted to include in your project.

You may also want to keep your book stored in a cloud-based app like DropBox. This lets you work from anywhere, so long as you have a data connection.

Stuck in line at the grocery store or waiting at your doctor's office? Pull up your book and add a few thoughts to your Work In Progress. Though they may not seem like much, these little moments can really add up and make it easier for you to reach your writing goals.

Resources to Help You Write Faster

Writing your book doesn't mean you have to come up with tons of brand new content. Most online entrepreneurs already have a large collection of material they can draw from, they just don't realize it. Before you start work on your book, roll up your sleeves and start looking through your archives.

Start with old blog posts or articles you've written previously. Is the information evergreen? Could you tweak it a little to fit with the theme of the book you're writing? Are there points in your article that you'd love to expand on?

If you find a few you like, then use those old blog posts. These can save you hours of time writing your content. Even if you decide to rewrite an old post, you'll still have the bones of your next chapter already outlined.

Don't stop with your blog posts, though. Look through your old podcast or radio episodes. Did you interview an expert and get some quotes that would be helpful to readers? Did your rant on a certain topic inspire your listeners to share their own thoughts? That's even more book fodder!

Once you're done with your podcasts, re-watch some of your old videos. These videos may be on websites like YouTube or Vimeo. Or perhaps, it's newer content that you recently shared in your Facebook Live videos.

Take notes as you watch so you'll know what you want to salvage from each podcast or video. Be sure to list the source for your own records *(e.g. from Facebook Live Video on 4/13/2017)*. This helps you save time if you need to review your previous content.

Next, look around at events in which you've participated. Did you give a popular presentation during a webinar? Was your speech at a local networking event met with rave reviews? Were people impressed by your information?

These are all signs that you shared some awesome content. You can use this content again while writing your book. However, if your content was part of someone else's event, you may need to talk to that person before you use your previous remarks.

Turn Your Story Into Cash: Writing & Launching Your Book

For example, if you were the presenter during a webinar for Jill, you could say, "Hey Jill! I had a blast doing the webinar with you last summer. With your blessing, I'd like to use this content in my upcoming book."

Most event hosts won't be bothered by the fact you're using previous content. In fact, they may be delighted to see you repurposing your awesome content to share with even more people.

Don't get bogged down by thinking you have to write hundreds of pages of new content. Instead, look around for resources you've already created and see if you can repurpose them for your upcoming book.

What Will You Outsource?

When it comes to publishing your own book, you can do everything yourself. You can choose to wear the hat of editor, cover designer, formatter, and web designer. But just because you can do everything yourself doesn't mean that's the best option.

It's always a good idea to bring in industry professionals who you know and trust. They can give you honest feedback about your book and point out key ways you can improve it. With their feedback, you can transform a ho-hum book into a must-read that climbs the charts of book sellers everywhere.

Now, you may be wondering who you should hire first. It's always a good idea to start with an editor. An editor can do so much more than simply suggest grammar and spelling changes.

Your editor can read your book looking for cohesiveness, making sure it flows smoothly from one thought to the next. Your editor can also give you insights into how to strengthen your writing and point out passages that are unnecessary or boring. Finally, your editor will polish your words, making sure your book is as entertaining as possible.

Once you've finished the editing phase of your book, it's time to hire another professional. This time you'll want to opt for a cover designer. Your cover is the best advertising platform you will ever buy. Many potential readers will decide whether or not to purchase your book based solely on the cover.

Planning Your Book and Launch

Don't outsource this task to a friend of a friend who's been experimenting with Photoshop. That's because you're not only paying a cover designer for the cover. You're also paying them for their years of experience and training. Often, cover designers can tell you exactly what mistakes to avoid when it comes to a cover and they can guide you on choosing the image that's most likely to appeal to your readers.

Once your cover is completed and you're happy with the final product, it's time to hire a formatter. Your book formatter will optimize your book so it looks good on different screen sizes and resolutions. If you choose to make print copies of your book available, your formatter can also make sure the book prints correctly.

Your formatter will make sure your fonts are consistent in size and style. She'll check that the page numbers are accurate and make sure each chapter begins on a new page. If you've included graphics or charts in your book, she'll ensure they display correctly.

Finally, you'll need to hire a website designer. Even if you already have a website, you should register the domain name for your book, too. This makes it easy for you to share the URL during networking events like conferences and seminars.

Ideally, your book website should contain a short blurb about your book, an excerpt, and links to where readers can buy your book. You also want a sign-up box so visitors can subscribe to your mailing list. With a mailing list in place, you can launch your next book and immediately message your subscribers to let them know about it. If your list is large, you can expect a few sales from doing this one promotional activity.

Marketing Your Book

Writing and launching your book is only the beginning. Now, it's time to sell your book to readers, a process known to authors as marketing. Marketing is making people aware of your book so they become engaged with your writing and buy it.

Your marketing plan needs a three-prong approach. The first prong is for short-term strategies. These are quick but short things you do to make your book visible. A week-long Facebook advertising campaign is an example of a short-term strategy. Other quick strategies might include:
- Hosting a book signing event

- Organizing a blog tour for your book
- Advertising your book release on Instagram
- Releasing a short podcast series about your book
- Announcing your launch in a Facebook Live video
- Sending out a press release to your local newspaper

The second prong of your marketing strategy should be long-term strategies. Often, these strategies don't result in a rush of buyers. They slowly build your author brand and cement you as a leader in your niche.

When you're focusing on long-term strategies, remember that many customers have to be shown a product several times before they make a purchase. This may mean that customers only start buying your book after your seventh email or maybe the twenty-fifth mention of it on social media. Some long-term strategies might include:
- Creating a book trailer and uploading it to video sites
- Building your list of email subscribers
- Giving away promotional items with your book title and website
- Nurturing a Facebook group of members who are in your target demographic
- Attending live networking events
- Teaching workshops or speaking at seminars

The final prong in your marketing plan should be networking with other authors. This isn't about getting other authors to buy your book. It's about growing your circle of influence and becoming friends with other writers.

As you develop these relationships, you'll find your writing friends promoting your books even though you didn't ask them. Of course, you should return the favor and promote other authors, too. Don't be afraid to do this—there's more than enough room in the world for more amazing books.

Marketing tasks can be daunting, but don't let it get you down. Create a weekly marketing plan and stay on track. If you have trouble coming up with fresh marketing ideas, you can ask your writing friends for support and inspiration.

Launch Day Tips & Tactics

You've spent weeks or months waiting for this day—the moment you launch your book out into the world and add the title 'author' to your bio. You may be tempted to kick back and take it easy for a couple of weeks.

Planning Your Book and Launch

But release day is actually one of the busiest days in an author's career. There are plenty of things you should be doing to market your brand-new book.

Start by uploading a book trailer to YouTube. You want your video on YouTube because it's the world's second most popular search engine. That means when people want recommendations for the next book they should buy, they start looking on Google, and then YouTube.

Once your book trailer is uploaded, start scheduling a Facebook party. Ideally, you want to do it within the next day or two. This helps create a bigger buzz about your book. Invite all of your friends to your party and encourage them to invite others they think may be interested.

You can kick off your event by doing a Facebook Live video. Facebook Live will promote your video for you, which can result in even more attendees at your party.

Interact with participants and host contests. For prizes, giveaway free promotional items like bookmarks, pens, or Amazon gift cards. You can also share some 'behind the scenes' information with attendees or host a Q & A session about your book's topic.

Another way to promote your book on launch day is to ask friends or colleagues if they'll interview you for their blog or podcast. This gives you a chance to showcase yourself as an expert while sharing about your new book. Contact Judi Moreo (702-283-4567) and ask her to review your book on her "World of Book Reviews" television show.

Don't forget to ask for reviews. Do this at your Facebook party and in your interviews. It's against most retailers' policies to ask for a good review. So, you might say, "If you enjoyed the book, please leave a review on (Amazon or Barnes and Noble or another site)."

There's a lot of hard work and hustle that goes into writing and publishing your book. Don't let the process overwhelm you. Take it one step at a time and keep going. You'll get to launch day if you keep chasing your dream.

Turn Your Story Into Cash: Writing & Launching Your Book

Checklist

Before you write your book, it's smart to slow down and do some research. This early research can help you craft a book that your audience will love and support.

Understanding Your Target Market

- [ ] **Determine the purpose of your book.** Think about what your goal is for writing and publishing this book, whether that's to attract new leads, establish your expertise, or earn additional revenue.
- [ ] **Identify your target audience.** If you don't have a clear audience in mind, you may need to do additional research about your niche.
- [ ] **Use keyword research to see what information your community is hungry for.** You can use a free keyword tool like Google's Keyword Tool to see which phrases your audience uses when searching online.
- [ ] **Go to Amazon and look for books about your topic.** Make a list of books that have high star ratings and are frequently recommended by reviewers.
- [ ] **Pay attention to gaps in the market.** These are areas other experts forget to cover within their books. When you spot gaps, make a note, as you may have stumbled across a profitable book idea.
- [ ] **Investigate the best-sellers list on Amazon.** The easiest way to do this is to go to a search engine like Google and type: "Amazon Best Sellers (Niche)" without quotation marks. You should replace the word niche with the niche you'll be writing about.
- [ ] **Study the covers of various best sellers.** Note which fonts are on these covers, what images are depicted, and which colors are most popular.
- [ ] **Check out the prices of the books on the best sellers list.** Look for the highest price, the lowest, and the average. This information will help you when it's time for you to publish your book.

Planning Your Writing Schedule

- [ ] **Write out what a typical day looks like for you.** Include all of your activities, both personal and professional.
- [ ] **Review your day.** Now that you know how you're spending your time, look for ways you could sneak some writing time in.
- [ ] **Look for tasks you could outsource if you're short on time.** You may be more productive if you employed a cleaning lady or hired a lawn care service.

Planning Your Book and Launch

- [ ] **Delegate what must be done.** Don't be afraid to delegate tasks to a significant other or an older teen. This will leave you more time to work on your book.
- [ ] **Give up a hobby temporarily.** Ask yourself what you could let go for a few weeks until your book is done. For example, you could avoid binge-watching your favorite shows on Netflix while you're working on your book.
- [ ] **Keep notes.** When you're writing a book, it's perfectly normal to have new ideas pop into your head. Use your smart phone to take notes or record your thoughts before you forget them.
- [ ] **Store your book in the cloud.** Use a cloud-based system like DropBox so you can access your book no matter where you are. This lets you add new insights and ideas into your book while you're waiting at the doctor's office or standing in line at the bank.

Tools for Writing Faster

- [ ] **Look through your old blog posts or articles.** If the content is evergreen and applies to your book, consider repurposing it. You may even have enough previous content to write entire chapters.
- [ ] **Dig through old podcasts or radio episodes.** It's easy to forget all of the helpful advice and great quotes you shared on your episodes. Give them a listen and see if there's some content you'd like to use again.
- [ ] **Watch your videos.** Check out your old videos on YouTube or re-watch your Facebook Live videos. Pay attention to content that would fit well with your book.
- [ ] **Review your previous events.** If you were a featured guest on a webinar or gave a speech at a local networking meeting, that's more content you could re-use. Keep in mind that you need to ask permission from the event host before you recycle this content.
- [ ] **Make notes as you come across old resources.** Jot down notes about where the content came from. This will help you when you need to look back to double-check details or want to make sure your facts are accurate.

Outsourcing Elements of Your Book

- [ ] **Find an editor.** Editing is an important job and your book deserves the time and attention from a professional. Make sure the editor is one you trust to do their very best work.
- [ ] **Get a professional cover designer.** Your cover is the first impression your

readers will have of your book and you want it to be a good one.
- [ ] **Invest in a book formatter.** A formatter does so much more than adjust font sizes or center text. A good formatter makes sure your book looks professional and polished.
- [ ] **Enlist a web designer.** Your book needs a website so you can help visitors discover your work. Be sure to have your web designer create links so readers can download your book on Amazon Kindle, Kobo, Barnes and Noble Nook, and iBooks.
- [ ] Contact Judi Moreo at judi@judimoreo.com for referrals for any help needed with Editing, Cover Design, Book Formatting, or Web Design.

Marketing Techniques

- [ ] **Offer a digital book signing.** There are plenty of sites where you can create digital autographs for your readers. One popular site that will help you do this is Authorgraph.com.
- [ ] **Advertise your book on Instagram.** If you know your target market loves Instagram, then use this to your advantage and advertise on the social platform.
- [ ] **Send a press release to your local newspaper.** If you live in a small city or town, write a press release and email it your editor. She might just print it!
- [ ] **Release a short podcast series about your book.** Keep the momentum and excitement around your book going by creating a podcast series. Your episodes can pick up where the book left off or they could contain behind-the-scenes info.
- [ ] **Network with authors.** Join online and offline writing groups. Participate in these forums and help support other writers. Your kindness will come back to you!

Embracing Launch Day

- [ ] **Upload your book trailer to YouTube.** Most consumers have embraced video and love getting to see promotional trailers about upcoming or newly released books.
- [ ] **Schedule a Facebook party.** Invite your friends, colleagues, and fans. Let them know they're welcome to invite others, so you can reach even more people.
- [ ] **Use Facebook Live.** Kick off your Facebook party with a live video. Share how excited you are and encourage attendees to stick around for prizes and bonus content.

Planning Your Book and Launch

- ☐ **Offer Prizes.** Giving away prizes is a quick way to keep people engaged at your party. You can ask for selfies and offer a prize to funniest selfie, the most serious selfie, or even the sexiest selfie.
- ☐ **Ask friends and colleagues to share your good news.** Have 2-3 preformatted Facebook posts that friends can copy and upload to their profiles.
- ☐ **Request reviews.** Let everyone at your party know how much you appreciate all reviews—whether good or bad. Invite them to share their thoughts on Amazon, Goodreads, or other book related websites.

Turn Your Story Into Cash: Writing & Launching Your Book

Worksheet

If you create a solid plan before you write and launch your book, then your odds of success are increased. Use this worksheet as the framework for your plan:

The purpose of my book is: _____.

My target audience is: _____.

My keyword research shows these are the terms my audience uses when searching online:
_____.

The top 5 best-selling books in my niche are:

1.

2.

3.

4.

5.

Planning Your Book and Launch

The gaps in my market include: _____.

The covers of the best-selling books in my niche have these things in common:

1.

2.

3.

4.

5.

The highest price for a book in my niche is:_____.

The lowest price for a book in my niche is: _____.

The average price for a book in my niche is: _____.

Section 2

Writing Your Book

When it comes to writing your book, it's easy to get overwhelmed. You may be looking at how many pages you need to fill or how many words you have to write to complete your book. Don't give up before you get started. There are plenty of ways you can break down this large goal into smaller, more achievable tasks. You can take the first steps toward writing your book by following this guide.

Create an Outline

An outline allows you to look at the overall vision you have for your book. It functions like a road map, showing you which path to take and highlighting milestones along the way.

The important thing to remember is your road map isn't set in stone. If you find something that interests you, it's fine to stop and spend some time examining it. You may discover that stopping to chase a tangent turned into your favorite chapter of your book.

If you do try something new or explore a story that doesn't fit with the rest of your book, you can always cut it out later. So, don't panic if you go off-track sometimes.

Before you begin mapping out your path, it can be helpful to define the premise of your book. You should be able to spell out what your book is about within a sentence or two. For example, the premise of John Green's popular novel, *The Fault in Our Stars*, could be summed up like this: Two terminally ill teens find love together.

The premise for a popular non-fiction book titled *The Life-Changing Magic of Tidying Up* by Marie Kondo would be: A cleaning consultant teaches readers how to organize their homes by focusing on what items bring them true joy.

Now that you have a couple of examples, spend a few minutes thinking about the premise of your book. Jot it down, and remember, you can always revise it later if you change the direction of your manuscript.

Once you're clear on your premise, it's time to start your outline. You can outline your book in a variety of ways but one of the easiest and most enjoyable ways to do this is to use sticky notes or index cards. When you use this method, it's easy to organize your thoughts.

You want to write down what you know will be part of your book. If you know that a funny story from your childhood will be the introduction for chapter three, put that on a note card. Keep adding ideas, putting each one on its own card.

When you've exhausted all of your ideas, tack up your notes or spread them out on a table or other hard surface. This is where you start looking for gaps and fill them in. For example, if you want to touch on your character's tragic back story before a pivotal scene, add a note mentioning that. If you want to talk about self-esteem boosters for kids in chapter four, make a note for that, too.

When you're done, you should have the bare bones of your book. You can go in during the writing process and add more details in each chapter. For now, you can use your notes as progress trackers to ensure you're covering every point you wanted to make.

Flesh Out Each Chapter

Once you have your outline, you're ready to get started writing your book. The best way to do this is to approach it one chapter at a time. When you think about writing a 200-page book, it feels like a huge undertaking. You may even be tempted to think, "I'll never write a book."

When you focus on completing one chapter at a time, it feels more doable. You're more likely to think, "A chapter's only 10 pages. I can do that!"

Since you've already outlined, you should have a rough idea of what you plan to cover. Take the time to slow down and really think about what you're writing. If you're starting your fiction novel with a meeting between two characters, take a moment and give a paragraph or two of back story about each one.

If your work is non-fiction and you're opening with a story from your life or a statistical reference, use a paragraph or two to paint the scene. Describe that story from your life or talk about where you were when you heard those stats for the first time.

As you write, it can be helpful to consider the 6W's. These are questions that every author should ask when they're writing. These questions include:
- What was/is going on?
- Who is there?
- Where is it happening?
- Why is this situation happening?
- When did/will it happen?
- What happens next?

Taking the time to answer these questions might feel tedious to you at first. However, they'll make your chapter much stronger and help your readers visualize what they're reading.

Another way to flesh out your writing is to use the five senses during a scene. The five senses include:
- Sight
- Smell
- Hearing
- Taste
- Touch

You want to include a minimum of three senses in each scene. So, if you start your book talking about your (or your character's) favorite summer memories, then mention the taste of popsicles, the smell of freshly cut grass, and the feel of hot pavement beneath bare feet. Including these details can make readers feel like they're actually in the scene.

Don't think that you have to start writing with the first chapter. Even the most talented authors sometimes find it hard to start with their first chapter. That's because it's the beginning and requires a lot of setup.

If you can't seem to make any progress with your book, feel free to skip around and start writing a different chapter. For example, you may want to start working on chapter 5 because that's the one that appeals to you right now. Don't ignore this urge.

Harness the creativity energy within you that's eager to write this chapter and get to work right now. Provided you have an outline and you're following it, you can write out of order without compromising your book.

Three Common Obstacles that Sideline Writers

You've started your book and you've put a few paragraphs down. As you're writing you feel great. But then, your writing session ends and you don't pull out your book again for a few days. You meant to write daily but something is stopping you.

You're struggling to think of your next sentence. You can't focus when you sit down to work. You may have even started to question whether you should create and launch a book, after all.

Before you give up and throw in the towel, you should know that what you're dealing with is normal. Writers, like all creatives, face three common obstacles. See if you recognize yourself in some of these obstacles:

Obstacle #1: Perfectionism

Every time you start to type a sentence, your inner editor cringes. You're terrified you're going to write something dreadful, so you don't write anything. You figure if you don't write, you'll never have to face the fact that your writing isn't perfect.

This mindset keeps you from growing. After all, you can't improve your writing until you've actually written something. Rather than staying chained to the belief your work must be perfect, focus on creating that first draft.

Give yourself permission to write a terrible book. When your inner editor criticizes you, remind her to wait her turn. She'll get her chance to point out flaws when it's time for you to do your revisions. In the meantime, keep writing.

Obstacle #2: Self-Doubt

Every writer struggles with self-doubt. You worry you've picked the wrong words. You worry no one will like your book. You worry that you don't have a natural talent for writing and you worry you're a great big fraud.

The way to overcome self-doubt is to write anyway. Letting self-doubt keep you from working on your book is like feeding a stray animal. That's because you're training self-doubt to come and eat your motivation. Self-doubt shows up because you've allowed it.

You need to stand up to self-doubt whenever he makes an appearance. No matter how loud he gets or how mean his insults, keep pushing through. Once you're in a good writing flow, he'll disappear and you'll be left alone to focus on your book.

Obstacle #3: Fear of Failure

Some authors call it "writer's block" when they can't seem to work on their books. In reality, writer's block is one way the fear of failure shows up in your life. You may think if you don't publish a book, you'll never have to suffer a bad review or an angry customer.

If you don't risk failure, you'll never gain anything. Without risking a negative review, you'll never get the 26 glowing reviews from readers. Without risking a few hours of your time, you'll never know if self-publishing is right for you.

You have to face down failure. You can't grow your career unless you're willing to take a few risks along the way.

Write in the face of every single obstacle—no matter how big or insurmountable that obstacle might seem. If you stay the course, you'll eventually get your book written and published. Just keep going.

How to Get Your Book Done Quickly

You're ready to get your book created and launched. You're excited about sharing it with the world and you want to write it quickly. Maybe you want this book off your plate before the end of the year. Maybe you want to launch it to coincide with a major holiday. Whatever your reason, you're fired up to get this done. Here are some creative ways you can write your book fast:

Attend a Writing Retreat

If your time and budget allow it, look up writing retreats in your state or country. You can find retreats where authors gather to get large portions of their books written. This motivation can rub off on you, allowing you to buckle down and write your chapters.

Another advantage of going on a writing retreat is that you're surrounded by other authors. That means if you run into a plot problem or need a fresh set of eyes to look over your opening chapters, you'll have a group of writers with whom you can brainstorm ideas.

Some authors have gone on retreats and come home with finished manuscripts and new friendships. It's possible that you might find your best writing friend while you're in the trenches together.

Take Vacation Days

If you work a job where you have paid vacation days, skip the beach and use your time to get your book written. This works best if you already have an outline and you're seriously committed to your book.

Of course, you have to be willing to guard your time. Friends and family may assume that since you're off, you can run errands, pick the kids up from day care, or landscape the whole lawn. You need to firmly tell people 'no'. You might say, "Yes, I'm on vacation, but this time has been earmarked for a personal project. Thanks for understanding!"

Go to a Hotel

Many well-known authors have written their books in hotel rooms. The advantage of staying at a hotel is that there's nothing to distract you from your work. When you're at home, you may be more likely to wash the looming pile of dishes and mow your overgrown lawn rather than write your book.

You don't have to break the budget and rent out the penthouse suite in a five-star hotel. It's fine to go to a small local hotel and sequester yourself until you've made some major progress on your book.

Hire a Sitter

If you have small kids, it can be nearly impossible to supervise them while working. That's where hiring a sitter can come in handy. You have someone to ensure the kids are cared for so you can focus all of your energy on your book.

Keep in mind you don't have to leave your house and go to a coffee shop. Many sitters will watch the kids while you're in the home office. This lets you get some work done and still be available in the event of a problem.

Finishing your book is important. Don't be afraid to make it a priority and find a creative solution to getting it done.

Keep Your Writing Time Productive

You've created space and time in your life for your book. You power up your laptop and sit down with a cup of coffee, determined to make some serious progress. Four hours pass and you glance at your document. You've written a grand total of 23 words. You feel terrible and wonder where all that time went.

You're not alone. Many writers struggle to keep their writing time productive. There are hundreds of distractions that can cripple your writing resolve. Here's how to beat them so you can get back to work on your book:

Start with your phone—that's where most people get the majority of their notifications. Put your phone on silent mode so you won't be aware of the dings and vibrations. If you're still tempted to pick it up and check notifications while you're writing, then you need to put your phone in a different room.

Don't stop with your phone, though. You should also turn notifications off in your inbox. There's no email so urgent that it can't wait until you've finished your writing for the day. Tell yourself that once you hit your writing goal, your reward will be a nice long email session.

If you cut off notifications and still end up wasting time online, then you need to do something drastic like blocking the internet. There are a variety of programs that you can use to do this.

Writing Your Book

One of the best is Cold Turkey. It will prevent you from accessing certain websites or even the entire internet for a specified period of time. If you can't seem to log out of Facebook or Twitter, then this app might be exactly what you need. It's even free to try so you can see how well it works.

Most writers need a lot of ambient noise in order to get their best work done. If you suspect this might be your problem, then try writing in a coffee shop and see if it makes you more productive and more focused. You could also try quiet locations like bookstores or libraries.

If you like working at different locations, be sure to take with you any material you may want to use while you work - like interviews or statistics. Don't forget to bring a copy of your outline with you so you can reference it, if needed.

Some people find they do their best work in high pressure situations. They're usually the ones who wait until a few hours before the deadline to work on a project. If that describes you, then it might be helpful to set a timer while you work.

Don't go easy on yourself. Set a tough challenge, like writing a thousand words in forty-five minutes. The pressure of trying to beat the timer mimics the feeling of having an important deadline and boosts your productivity.

Keep notes on what works best for your productivity. This will give you a list of solutions next time you find yourself feeling like you just can't write.

Is Accountability the Missing Ingredient for You?

One reason some writers struggle to write and launch a book is because they're the only one who knows about their goal. So, they don't have anyone or anything pushing them to succeed. This makes it easy to spend four hours playing video games or waste three hours on Facebook and other distractions.

Maybe you can relate. You tell yourself that you meant to work on your book but you got distracted by so many other things. If that describes you, then what you really need is some form of accountability.

After all, it's easy to let yourself off the hook when you're the only who knows about your goal. When other people know, it creates a type of pressure that forces you to work. That's because you don't want to disappoint those around you. Here's how to use accountability to keep pushing yourself forward:

Tell a friend how many words you'll write today.

Send your friend an email or text message that you'll be writing XX number of words today. Ask him to follow up with you at a certain time. For example, you might write, "I'm working on chapter five of my book today. I need to write 1,000 words to finish up. Can you text at 8 o'clock tonight and ask me what my word count is?"

Then get to work as soon as you send the message. Even if your friend forgets about the text, you still won't want to let him know you didn't accomplish your goal.

Co-work with another writer.

If you know another writer who's also working hard to write a book, arrange a get-together. You can meet at a local coffee shop or library and work on your projects together.

If your friend is online, you could do a Skype session or a Google Hangout. Stay on call as you work together. This gives you instant accountability and keeps you productive, even if you don't feel like writing.

Make a Public Commitment

Another way to become accountable is to announce your plan to write and publish your book publicly. Share about it on your blog and promote that post like crazy so everyone sees it. Make a big announcement on your next podcast episode and give yourself a deadline.

Boost your motivation to get your work done by going public with it. You don't want to tell all of your subscribers and listeners that you spent your time goofing off and that's why your book launch is being delayed.

Hire a Writing Coach

If you've tried everything else and nothing seems to be working, it might be time to hire a writing coach. A writing coach will listen to your ideas, give you feedback, and help you brainstorm when you're stuck. Judi Moreo is a good choice. (702) 283-4567

One thing a writing coach won't do is put up with your excuses. He or she will call you on them. You'll be challenged to keep working on your book, regardless of what's going on around you and encouraged to keep at it until you're done.

If you haven't been working on your book lately, pick one of the accountability methods mentioned above. Then implement that suggestion and start writing!

Capturing the Elusive Beginning

If there's one area of a book that trips up writers, it's the beginning. That's because you're smart enough to know that the beginning of your book has to hook a reader. You have to say something so profound, so funny, or so interesting that your audience can't help but buy your book. This can create a lot of pressure and stress you out. Here's how to cope:

You don't have to settle on the first beginning that you write. A director wouldn't watch only one actor audition for a part. He'd want to see a lot of different actors and only then would he start narrowing down his choices.

You can do the same thing with your beginnings. Write several opening paragraphs and keep in mind that you can always extend auditions and keep searching until that perfect beginning walks in and wows you.

Start your book in the middle of an action sequence. For example, you're writing about a doctor who saves the life of a teenage girl, only to discover later that the girl is the daughter he never knew he had. Don't open your book with three paragraphs about how the doctor woke up and went through his usual daily routine. That's not captivating.

Instead, start with the moment the doctor sees the nearly lifeless girl on the gurney. Write about how his heart pounds and adrenaline kicks in as he fights to save her. That's a good action sequence and it will intrigue your readers.

If your book is non-fiction, you can still lead with a captivating story. Once your reader is hooked, you'll have plenty of time to share background information and weave in additional details. For now, focus on the action.

Not sure a story's the way to go? Try starting with a quote instead. This can be a quote that inspires you or one that sums up the chapter to come.

Turn Your Story Into Cash: Writing & Launching Your Book

You can also try using a humorous quote to make your readers laugh, but keep in mind this may not be appropriate for all books.

If you're having trouble finding quotes, use a quote directory. Two good ones are Brainy Quote and Quotelicious. You can use the search bar to find a specific quote if you know the author or you can browse by topic.

Another way to start your book is to write about a conversation taking place and go from there. However, try to keep your conversation limited to just 2-3 characters. Remember, your readers are learning who's who, so you don't want to risk confusing them.

Make sure the conversation is interesting and not mundane. Two men outside a diner discussing the weather will result in a bland scene. But if those two men are discussing how to get away with murder, then the conversation is naturally more intriguing.

Keep experimenting with different openings. If you continue to write, you'll eventually find the beginning you truly love.

Mastering the Ending of Your Book

Your readers have stuck with you throughout your book. They're delighted by your work and they can't wait to see how it all ends. This is crunch time for an author. It's the moment when you'll make the biggest impact on a reader.

If you choose an ending that's weak and boring, your reader may not remember your book or your name after they finish. If you choose an ending that doesn't fit, your reader may end up angry and refuse to read more of your books.

The ending of your book needs to be strong and conclusive. It should cement your name and your words in the minds of readers. Here's how to finish strong:

Try Ending with a Teaser

One popular way to end a book is to use a teaser ending. This is when the author intentionally leaves out vital information so readers feel compelled to pick up the next book. This can work well for fiction authors who have mapped out an entire series. It's not a good choice for non-fiction books, as readers will feel cheated.

Go Back to the Beginning

Sometimes, the best way to end a book is to remind the reader of how far the story's come. For example, your book focuses on family legacies. You opened the book with the hero's father committing a violent crime and going to prison. When you end the book, the hero is choosing a life of crime, just like his father.

The Sad Ending

Not every book needs to end on a positive note. In fact, it can be powerful to have an ending that's sad or unsettling. However, don't give your book a sad ending just because you want to.

Your sad ending should feel natural, like the story is unfolding the way it should. If you force a sad ending, readers are likely to feel cheated and will be angry with you. When you plan to end on a sad note, use foreshadowing so readers can sense early on that things won't end well.

The Happily Ever After Ending

Sometimes, the right ending for a book is a happy one. You or your characters have triumphed over obstacles to get to their happy moment. It's easy to gloss over the moment and hurriedly finish up your book.

Slow down and give your characters time to appreciate where they are. Readers will savor this moment and finish your work on a happy note. This makes them more likely to pick up your next book and start reading it!

Writing a book isn't an easy feat. But it can be done. Keep at it and you'll one day find yourself happily typing the words 'The End'.

Turn Your Story Into Cash: Writing & Launching Your Book

Checklist

Writing a book can be fun, but it can also be frustrating. You can avoid some of these frustrations and problems by following the checklist below.

Outlining Your Book

- [ ] **Identify your premise.** Basically, you need to decide what happens in your story and to whom it happens. Try to keep your premise simple. You should be able to explain it in a sentence or two.
- [ ] **Outline using note cards.** Note cards or sticky notes are perfect for jotting down ideas. Put one idea or one scene on each card.
- [ ] **Write down what you know.** Everything you know about your book so far should be on a card. This makes it easy to see your story visually.
- [ ] **Spread out your cards.** Once you've written down everything you know, put your cards on a table or other sturdy surface.
- [ ] **Fill in gaps.** Now, look through your book for gaps or holes. Take new cards and add more ideas to fill in these spots. This process can take a couple of hours, so be sure to give yourself lots of time.

Bulking Up Your Chapters

- [ ] **Focus on one chapter at a time.** Don't think about how long your book has to be or how many words you need to write. Concentrate on working on a single chapter.
- [ ] **Paint the opening scene.** Describe what's happening and why it's important. If the opening isn't important, then it's probably not the true beginning of your book.
- [ ] **Include the five senses as you write.** The more senses you include during your scenes, the more the readers will feel like they're experiencing it.
- [ ] **Skip around if you can't get the beginning down.** Sometimes, you can't seem to get your beginning right. If that's happening to you, don't sweat it. Write a different scene.

Overcoming Writing Obstacles

- [ ] **Remind yourself the first draft doesn't have to be perfect.** It's OK to make mistakes and mess up. That's what revisions are for!
- [ ] **Push through self-doubt.** You can do this by setting a clock for 10 minutes and saying that's all the time you have to write. You can also ask

yourself to just write one paragraph. Soon, you'll get in the writing zone and forget all about your self-doubt.
- [ ] **Focus on writing the best book you can.** Don't concentrate on your fear of failing. Encourage yourself to stick with it by doing your very best work.

Getting Your Book Written Quickly

- [ ] **Go on a writing retreat.** A retreat can be a great way to break out of your routine and write a big chunk of your book.
- [ ] **Hire a baby sitter.** It's hard to work with little ones in the room. Get a baby sitter so you can write in peace for a couple of hours.
- [ ] **Take a few vacation days.** If you have paid vacation days where you work, consider taking some time off to focus on finishing your book.
- [ ] **Hang out at a hotel.** If you struggle to write when you're at home, then change up your location by going to a hotel for a few days.

Keeping Your Writing Sessions Productive

- [ ] **Put your phone in silent mode.** Your phone is an enemy to productivity, so turn it off or at the very least on silent until you can get some words written.
- [ ] **Turn off your email notifications.** Do you really need to be notified every time you get a spam message? Probably not. Kill the notifications while you're working.
- [ ] **Block the internet.** Some writers will procrastinate if they can connect to the internet. If that's you, try using an app that blocks your access to the internet for a brief period.
- [ ] **Work at different locations.** If ambient noise helps you get things done, then try writing at a local coffee shop, library, or bookstore.
- [ ] **Set a timer.** Some writers find they can only be productive in a high-pressure situation. Recreate this feeling by setting a timer and giving yourself a tight deadline, like writing 700 words in 20 minutes.

Using Accountability to Get Your Book Done

- [ ] **Tell a friend or colleague how many words you'll write today.** You don't want to look bad in front of your friends and colleagues, so this is a sure-fire way to get those words down on paper.
- [ ] **Co-work with another author.** Sometimes, productivity is as simple as having another writer around you. Meet up at a coffee shop or park and

focus on knocking out a big chunk of your book.
- ☐ **Make a public commitment.** Shout from the rooftops about your upcoming book. Let everyone on social media and your blog know that you're writing and publishing a book.
- ☐ **Hire a writing coach.** Some writers need the discipline that comes from having a coach who keeps them accountable. If nothing else has worked, a writing coach may be what you need. Judi Moreo is an excellent writing coach. You can contact her at (702) 283-4567

Capturing the Elusive Beginning

- ☐ **Audition different beginnings.** No one says you have to stick with one beginning. You can write multiple beginnings until you find one that works for your book.
- ☐ **Start with an action sequence.** Jump right into your book with some fast-paced or suspenseful action that will keep readers' attention.
- ☐ **Lead with a captivating story.** Sometimes, the best way to begin is to start with a thrilling tale that intrigues your readers.
- ☐ **Begin with a quote.** This can be a funny or serious quote. Choose one that will interest readers and make them want to know more.
- ☐ **Use dialogue to open your book.** When you use this method, you need to quickly identify who is talking and what's happening to avoid any confusion for readers.

Mastering the Ending of Your Book

- ☐ **End with a teaser.** If your book is part of a series and you want readers to rush out and grab your next book, then end on a hook. Do this carefully—sometimes, it angers readers.
- ☐ **Circle back to the beginning.** A book that ends the same way it began can be powerful and gripping.
- ☐ **Try a sad conclusion.** Sometimes, there's no way to end on a happy note. Maybe an important character failed to achieve his goal or maybe he died. If this is the case, don't feel like you have to make everything all smiles by the end.
- ☐ **Go for the happily ever after ending.** If you or your character achieved your goals and are now enjoying a better life, then the happy ending might be the best fit for your book.

Writing Your Book

Worksheet

My book will have _____ chapters.

Each chapter needs to be _____ pages long.

My genre is: _____.

The premise of my book is: _____

_____

_____.

I know these events, topics, or scenes will appear in my book:

1.

2.

3.

4.

5.

I could start my book with these scenes or events:

1.

- Who:
- What:
- Where:
- Why:
- When:
- What happens next:

2.

- What do you see:
- What do you smell:
- What do you hear:
- What do you taste:
- What do you feel:

3.

4.

5.

Writing Your Book

I'll keep my writing time productive by: _____
_____
_____.

To reach my daily or weekly word count, I'll be accountable to:
_____
_____.

In order to write and publish a book, I'll give these activities up:
_____
_____.

Section 3

Publishing Your Book

You've done the hard work of writing and editing your book and now you're ready for the next step—publishing! Publishing your book means making it available for the public to read and review. Now's not the time to slack off.

You may now discover that writing your book was the easy part. Publishing it is sometimes difficult because you have to make dozens of tiny decisions along the way. Here's what you need to know to start on your path to publication:

Why Self-Publishing Is Awesome

Decades ago, if a writer wanted to publish a book, she had to submit it to agents and editors. She could only hope they'd love her manuscript and deem it worthy of publication. If she couldn't find anyone in publishing to take on her book, that was the end. Her dream was over unless she started working on a new book that would hopefully appeal to an editor.

Now with the invention of the internet and the rise of self-publishing technology, an author can publish her own work. That means even if you've been rejected by gatekeepers at traditional publishers, you can still get your work out there.

The best part is readers love indie authors who produce their own work. They love supporting an artist's dream and getting to be part of your journey. If you keep at it, you can build a large community filled with readers who believe in your work.

Publishing Your Book

Another perk of self-publishing is you get to keep all of your own earnings. This may surprise you, but most traditional authors only make a few cents per book sold.

In order to sell books, publishers have to offer deep discounts to booksellers. After the discounts, the publishing house gets their cut of the author's paycheck. This can be as much as 80% of the purchase price.

Then, the author's agent gets a cut of the remaining funds. A typical agent fee is 15% of the earnings. That means by the time the author is paid, they see about 5% of the profits.

Imagine what you could do if you saw 95% of your earnings. You could afford to quit your job and spend your days writing. You could focus on your marketing directly to the masses without worrying that a publisher is going to eat you for lunch.

Not only do you earn more when you self-publish, you also have total control over your book. Traditional authors often have to compromise when it comes to working with a publisher. This may mean they have to cut a beloved scene from their book or re-work the ending if an editor tells them it needs to be changed.

Authors also have very little control over their covers. Since covers can make or break the success of a book, this is a big deal. If a publishing house chooses a cover that's ugly or doesn't appeal to the target audience, the author is stuck with it. When that book doesn't sell well, the author will be blamed, no matter how wonderful her prose is.

You don't want that. You want to be free to make your own decisions. After all, you wrote your book, so you know it best. You know how to market it and how to weave a twist into your ending page that will shock and delight your fans. You know how to pick a cover that will make buyers drop everything to read your book.

If you approach it with the right attitude, self-publishing can be an awesome adventure. It can change your life and give you a deeper purpose.

Who to Hire When You Self-Publish

So, you've decided to skip the traditional publishing route, at least for now. You want to be in charge and make all of the important decisions when it comes to your book.

There is one tiny advantage that traditionally published authors have over you – a traditionally published author has a team of talented people behind their books. This evens out the workload and makes it easier for you to focus on growing your career as an author.

The good news is you can build your own team of professionals to help your book get the attention and praise it deserves. Here are four key members you'll want on your side as you self-publish your book:

A Professional Editor

Hiring a professional editor is different than working with one at a publishing house. A publisher's editor will recommend changes and additions to your work. For the most part, you have to implement their changes. Otherwise, you'll get a reputation as an author who is difficult to work with.

When you hire a professional editor, it's a different experience. You don't have to change your ending or edit out the humorous scene you included in your book. That's because you're working together as equals. You can implement the advice from your editor that you agree with and ignore the advice you don't.

A Publishing Coach

A publishing coach can be an invaluable member of your team. Your coach will encourage you and give you accountability. If you say you'll have five chapters edited by the end of the week, your coach will follow up with you. She'll make sure you're doing the work you say you are, so you can reach your publishing dreams.

Not only will your coach keep you on track during your editing phase, a good coach can also guide you through the publishing journey. She can point out pitfalls and help you avoid beginner mistakes. She can make recommendations based on your target market and your goals. She'll help you grow as an author, so you can have a long, successful career in publishing.

Publicity Manager

A publicity manager isn't the same as a publishing coach. While a coach works with you to write and publish your book, your publicity manager helps you market that book. He can do things for you like setting up a blog tour, getting you interviewed on popular podcasts, and sending review copies to top industry names.

When it comes to hiring a publicity manager, there are two key things you should look at. First, examine past clients. If your manager has helped a few indie authors become household names, then you're working with someone that's a true professional.

Second, pay attention to how well you like the publicity manager. You'll be working closely with this person for months, or even years, to come. So, make sure your personalities are a good fit. If they aren't, you're better off ending things early rather than trying to put up with someone you don't like.

A Virtual Assistant

As your career grows, it's going to require more of your time and attention. This can be a good thing, but you also have other important responsibilities in your life - like your friends, family, and job.

You don't want to be that author who's a stranger to everyone she loves because she's constantly working. That's where a virtual assistant can come in. The truth is, not every task must be handled directly by you.

You can let your VA send out review copies to bloggers and website owners. You can also get her to manage your inbox and social media accounts. This keeps your platform growing while you're busy writing your next book.

Don't be afraid to surround yourself with smart professionals. The more people you have working with you, the higher your chances of success.

How to Self-Publish

When it comes to self-publishing, there are dozens of books and resources available. With so much information about the topic, it's easy to get overwhelmed before you even begin your publishing adventure. Don't give up. Here's a simple overview of what the self-publishing journey looks like.

Polish Your Book

Some authors are so excited about sharing their book with the world that they write the words 'The End' and immediately upload their manuscript for publication. Then, the reviews start coming in and they see a lot of negativity.

Reviewers complain that fonts changed throughout the book, that pages aren't formatted correctly, and there are too many typos. You don't want this to happen to your book. That's why you must take the time to polish your manuscript.

You can start polishing it by getting a good editor to look over your book. After an editor has looked over your book and you've implemented her advice, find a proofreader. Your proofreader will catch typos and other mistakes in your book.

Find a Cover Designer

As you're working to edit and polish your book, start thinking about your cover. Look up the Amazon best seller lists for your genre. Look at the different covers and see if you can spot similarities or patterns. This can give insight into what prompts visitors to become buyers.

Once you have a few ideas, reach out to a cover designer. Look for a designer who specializes in creating books for your genre. A designer who creates horror covers isn't going to be the best choice for your cute girly cover.

Format Your Book

Now that you have a cover and your book is completely edited, it's time to get a book formatter. Don't pick just anybody for this task. You want someone that specializes in book formatting so that your final work looks polished and professional.

Keep in mind that you need your book available in a variety of formats. That means you may have to pay your formatter several times, depending on the number of formats you need.

Publishing Your Book

Don't skip this step. If you try to upload a book that isn't the right format, it will look terrible when it's published and reviewers will complain. Do this right the first time and you won't have to worry about it again.

If you find publishing is overwhelming you, slow down and take it one task at a time. It's better to make slow progress than no progress.

Digital Downloads

When it comes to self-publishing, there's a lot of debate about which platforms you should use. Right now, the top three platforms where you can publish your books are Amazon Kindle, Kobo, and iBooks. All of these platforms are unique in that customers shop differently on each one. If you understand this, then you can use it to your advantage.

Amazon Kindle

On Amazon Kindle, most buyers are looking for a good deal. That means you may want to price your book for $2.99 then offer it on sale for $0.99 for a few days each month. This can really boost your sales and help you hit some of those best seller lists.

Amazon also has a special program for their authors called Kindle Direct Publishing. With KDP, you can earn up to 70% royalties on the purchase price of the book. However, your book is exclusive to Amazon during this period and can't be sold elsewhere.

Some authors have used KDP with great success. Others have self-published their books on Amazon without opting to be exclusive and have seen great success. KDP won't necessarily make or break your career.

However, there is a big drawback to using KDP. It puts all of your earnings in one platform. What happens if Amazon decides to suspend your author account? You've lost all of your royalties and you'll be hustling to get your book selling on other sites.

Kobo

Kobo is a popular online bookstore in Canada. For Kobo, many of their buyers are binge readers. They want big boxed sets of books (think three or more books per product) and they're willing to pay a lot more than Amazon readers. If you plan on publishing multiple books, especially as a series, then you'll definitely want to check out Kobo.

Another advantage of Kobo is it offers helpful statistics to readers. For example, it displays how long it will take for you to read a book or a series. This can be helpful for readers heading out for vacation who want to load up their e-reader with some new titles.

iBooks

iBooks is Apple's publishing platform. With iBooks, you can set your books up for pre-order a year in advance. This gives you plenty of time to tease readers with short excerpts, cover reveals, and more.

You can also price a book for $9.99 or more, if you choose to. Use this feature if you plan on publishing books that are highly detailed on a topic that's not well-known.

For example, if you notice that no one has published a clear instruction manual for a certain computer language, then write the book and upload it to iBooks. Set the price higher than you would for other books, since you're leading the niche.

Unless you're considering using Amazon's exclusive KDP program, don't feel like you have to choose. You can use all three platforms to sell your books. Best of all, each platform comes with plenty of statistics for authors that you can use to grow your brand.

Your Print-On-Demand Options

In addition to self-publishing your book on platforms like Kindle, iBooks, and Kobo, you may also want to consider using print on demand technology. Print on demand is ideal for books that customers may wish to have a physical copy of, like a children's bedtime story, a special workbook, or a beautiful journal. Here's how it works:

You upload a copy of your manuscript to a print on demand service like Create Space or Lulu. When a customer purchases a tangible copy of your book, the service prints it and sends it to the buyer.

The advantage of print on demand is that there is no minimum order. In previous decades, if you wanted a tangible copy of your book you had to

Publishing Your Book

order a minimum number of books in order to cover the printing price. This figure could be as much as 500-5,000. If you couldn't sell all of the books you had to order, you were stuck with a huge inventory.

But now, print on demand technology lets you print one or two copies at a time. This means you don't have to make a huge up-front investment or worry about having 600 copies of your book and not being able to sell all of them.

Another advantage of using print on demand services is that it's free to do. If you've already hired an editor and formatter, you can simply take your book and upload to the website of your choice. Of course, if you find you need additional help, many companies will offer services like cover design or editing for a small fee.

Some print on demand companies will also give you a free ISBN. If you're not familiar with the term, an ISBN is an international standard book number. Having an ISBN means your book is cataloged in the millions of print and e-books available around the world.

Of course, you need a separate ISBN for each version of a book. For example, your print book will have a different ISBN than your digital e-book. By using an ISBN from your printing company, you'll save time and money.

If you expect that you'll get most of your sales from tangible copies of your book, you can upload it to a site like Create Space. Since the site is owned by Amazon, you can have your book uploaded to Amazon automatically. Then if your customers want a digital copy instead, they can easily find that.

Don't pick a print on demand company simply because they have the best deal. You want to work with a print on demand service that you like and that will give your buyers a great customer service experience.

Self-Publishing Mistakes to Avoid

Making a mistake when you're self-publishing can at best cause you some embarrassment. At worst, it can make your buyers flee before they even have a chance to get to know your book. This results in lost sales and if you're not aware of the mistake, it can leave you wondering why no one is raving about your book. Here's what to watch out for:

Turn Your Story Into Cash: Writing & Launching Your Book

Your cover isn't readable.

You did the cover yourself or had a friend with a little bit of Photoshop experience make it for you. The result is a lackluster cover that's not easy to read. Try viewing the cover as a thumbnail or about 150 pixels wide. Can you clearly read the title or does it blend in with the image? Do you know what the book is about based on the image or is the image too distorted to see?

If your cover looks terrible when it's small, it's time to take action. Most of your buyers will be viewing your book on a small tablet or smart phone. This means all they'll see is your tiny preview and if that cover isn't intriguing, they won't click through. They'll buy someone else's book.

Your author info isn't available.

Readers want to get to know the author behind a book. That means you need to have a professional head shot and a bio uploaded to your book's platform. You should also have a link to your website where readers can go to learn more about you.

Without a bio and picture, many platforms won't promote your book as frequently. This can slow sales even more. If you absolutely hate writing about yourself, get a copywriter to help. Keep working on this task until you come up with a bio that captures who you are and what you love writing about.

Your book description is too vague.

When it comes to your book description, you need to have two to three paragraphs that capture what your book is about. If you're too vague, readers will worry that your book isn't all that interesting or that it lacks a plot.

Try looking at other books in your genre and read their descriptions. If you're really struggling with this step, you could ask a fellow author or two for advice. Authors love supporting each other and will often share their own thoughts if you're brave enough to ask.

Your book has too much filler at the beginning.

Your cover looks fantastic. You filled out your author info and your book description is fantastic. You're getting a lot of readers that are requesting a free sample but no one's buying. You're left wondering where you went wrong.

Take a look at the front of your book and consider how much filler content you have. For example, a book that begins with a prologue, cast of characters, a dedication page, a map of your characters' home town, and three pages of praise doesn't leave any time for your readers to actually sample your work.

If you think the front of your book might have too much content, try downloading a sample. See how much of your book you actually get to read. If you only have one to two pages of book content, then you'll want to move some of your information to the back of the book. Link to your table of contents and trust that readers who are curious will use it, if needed.

Promoting Your Book Before the Release

In all of the excitement of publishing your book, it can be easy to get wrapped up in the details and forget to come up with a promotion plan. A promotion plan helps you pace yourself, so you don't try to accomplish all of your marketing tasks in a single afternoon.

Instead, you should use a promotional plan that allows you to consistently market your book. This keeps your work at the front of customers' minds and helps them anticipate your release. Here are a few tasks you'll want to make sure you include in your promo plans:

Send Out ARCs

If you're not familiar with the term, it stands for Advanced Reading Copies. These are special copies of your book sent out four to eight weeks before your release day.

The goal of sending out ARCs is so that you have a few people reviewing your book as soon as it releases. This can help you sell more books because visitors see these reviews and are more likely to take a chance on your book.

Don't send out ARCs and ask for five-star reviews. That can be seen as unprofessional in some circles. Instead, ask those receiving ARCs to post their honest thoughts about the book, whether good or bad.

Turn Your Story Into Cash: Writing & Launching Your Book

Organize a Blog Tour

Many book bloggers will review your book and post about it on their blog if you send them a free copy. When you send your book, let them know when your release day is and thank them for any support they can give. Be sure you're picking bloggers that read in your genre.

If you give a copy of your steamy romance to a young adult site owner, she may not feel comfortable posting about your book. Focus on bloggers that read in your niche and if you have doubts, contact the blogger before you send anything. Ask if they'd like a copy or if they'd prefer to pass.

Create a Media Kit

Make it easy for bloggers and reviewers to promote you. Create a special page on your website and name it 'Media Kit' or 'Media'. On this page, include your biography, a professional head shot, a blurb about your book, a high-resolution copy of your book cover, and the buy link to your book. Ideally, give your audience a link to your book on Kindle, iBooks, and Kobo.

As your platform grows, you'll need to expand this media kit to include information about your other books. But for now, this should be enough content so promoters can copy and paste to their websites or blogs.

Get Endorsements

If you have a few author friends, reach out and see if they'll give you an endorsement. Most authors will want to read a copy of your book before they're willing to publicly endorse your book, so be prepared to provide your book in a range of formats, if needed.

If you know an author who's willing to endorse a book without reading it, you may want to steer clear. A writer can get a bad reputation when all of her endorsements are from authors who promote every book under the sun.

Remember that marketing your book isn't a sprint. It's a marathon that will take you months to complete, so pace yourself and enjoy the journey.

Celebrating Release Day

After months of hard work, it's finally here: release day! You're thrilled and also a little bit nervous. Today is the day your dream has become reality: you're officially an author. How will you celebrate this awesome day?

Start by taking the day off.

If possible, take the day off from your responsibilities. Knowing your book has released will distract you and make it hard for you to be productive, because you'll want to check on your book every two minutes.

You may also have to deal with technical issues. For example, what if your book shows up on every platform but Amazon? You'll need to stop and deal with this issue immediately so you don't risk losing out on sales.

Throw a (virtual) party.

Try to schedule an online party for your release. You can use a social media site tool like Facebook Events to do this. Aim to schedule your party in the evening since many people are off work in the evenings. This allows more people to attend.

When scheduling, be mindful of time zones. If you throw a party at seven in the morning EST, it will be four in the morning on PST. This can make it difficult for people to attend and interact with you.

Keep It Light and Fun

Start by going live and introducing yourself and your book. During your party, invite your attendees to participate. You could have attendees post a picture of their favorite movie, share a tattoo they have, or post a silly selfie.

Thank Your Supporters

Look around at your support team. Who helped you get this far? Was it the support of your spouse? Did your writing coach spur you on? Who talked you through that plot hole or challenged you to keep going?

Now's the time to thank these supporters for all they've done and continue to do. By thanking these people, you're putting good karma out there and that's sure to come back to you.

Turn Your Story Into Cash: Writing & Launching Your Book

Publishing your book is hard work and you should feel proud of yourself! You've done something that most people only dream about. You had the determination and the willpower to stick with your book and get it done. It's time to celebrate...

Checklist

Now that you've written and edited your book, you've made it to the most exciting stage, publishing! There's a lot you need to do during this time, so use this checklist to make sure you don't forget anything.

Hiring a Team to Help When You Self-Publish

- [ ] Pay for a professional editor. When it comes to hiring an editor, you get what you pay for. Don't choose an editor because her rates are cheap. Instead, focus on picking one that's professional and comes highly recommended.
- [ ] Sign up for a publishing coach. Having a publishing coach on your side can ease your mind and help you make sense of the dozens of decisions that come with publishing your first book.
- [ ] Hire a publicity manager. There are hundreds of ways you can promote your book, but there's only one of you. To stay on top of the latest promotional trends and get your book in front of more readers, hire a publicity manager.
- [ ] Get a virtual assistant. During publishing, you'll have more tasks on your plate than ever before. Having a virtual assistant who will step in and help you manage your workload can be a life (and sanity!) saver.

Self-Publishing Your Book

- [ ] Polish your book. It's not enough to just have great writing. You also want to make sure your book is as polished and professional as it can be. Don't rush the polishing process. Take time to give your book the attention it deserves.
- [ ] Find a cover designer. Don't pick the first cover designer that comes along. Instead, choose one that specializes in your genre and understands what makes a successful book cover.
- [ ] Check the formatting of your book. After your book formatter has finished your book, go over it one last time. Make sure the margins are correct, the spacing is visually pleasing, and the chapters are in the right font.

Understanding Digital Platforms

- [ ] Upload your book to Amazon Kindle. This publishing program is most popular in the United States and has a reader base in the millions, mak-

- [ ] ing it the best platform to use for publishing an ebook.
- [ ] Submit to Kobo. Kobo is popular in Canada and the preferred way many readers there download content. If you want to appeal to Canadian readers, then publishing on Kobo is a must.
- [ ] Don't forget iBooks. iBooks is the reader app available through Apple. You'll need special software or a mac computer in order to upload your book to iBooks. If you don't have this software, you can use a third-party publisher like Draft 2 Digital to have your book uploaded to iBooks.

Looking at Your Print on Demand Options

- [ ] Use a Trusted POD publisher. There are plenty of POD publishers that will take advantage of new authors. That's why you should use a trusted name like Create Space or Lulu to create tangible copies of your book.
- [ ] Ask about minimum orders. Some POD publishers have a minimum order of a few hundred books. This can be financially risky, so ask about it before you sign any contracts or agree to any terms.
- [ ] Get an ISBN. POD Publishers will sometimes offer you a free International Standard Book Number. If yours does, be sure to take them up on the offer, as this can make it easier to get your book discovered.
- [ ] Order an advance copy. Once your book is uploaded to the POD company, request an advanced or galley copy. This allows you to preview how your book will look and feel for readers who order the tangible book.

Avoiding Self-Publishing Mistakes

- [ ] The cover is readable. Your cover needs to be readable at a small resolution, the size of a thumbnail or about 150 pixels wide. If your cover isn't readable in a small size, then it needs to be redone.
- [ ] Your author info is filled out and current. Take a few minutes to upload a photo of yourself and a biography. Doing this helps readers get to know you and makes it more likely they'll purchase your book.
- [ ] Your book description is clear and intriguing. If your book is amazing but your book description is a hot mess, then you aren't likely to get a lot of sales. Ask a copywriter to take a look at your description and share her thoughts.
- [ ] Your sample showcases your writing. Some authors put so much content at the front of their books that readers who download a sample never get to see their writing. Only put your title page, copyright notice, and your table of contents at the front of your book.

Promoting Your Book Before the Release

- [ ] Send out ARCs. ARCs are advanced reader copies that are sent to reviewers and bloggers ahead of the publishing date. You want to do this so you have a few reviews when your book finally goes live.
- [ ] Organize a blog tour. Try to appear on as many book blogs as you can within the first 7-14 days of your book release. This drives more traffic to your book, which raises your rankings so more readers learn about your new book.
- [ ] Create a media kit. Make sure it contains a high-resolution head shot of you, a brief biography, and a blurb about your book. Keep your media kit in a visible place so bloggers and website owners can easily feature you.
- [ ] Get endorsements. Reach out to some of your author friends and ask them to say something nice about your book. Most authors will request a copy of your book so they can review it first. Be prepared with free copies in advance.

Celebrating Release Day

- [ ] Take the day off. It's hard to concentrate when you have a book releasing and others are helping you promote it. Instead, take the day off from your regular life and plan to spend a lot of your time online.
- [ ] Throw a virtual party. It takes a village to publish a book, so invite everyone you know to celebrate with you. Better yet, get your friends to invite their friends, too!
- [ ] Keep it light. Now is the time to kick back and let loose. Keep your party fun and offer plenty of prizes to attendees.
- [ ] Thank your supporters. Don't forget to show your gratitude to everyone who helped along the way. If possible, send your supporters a small gift like a box of specialty chocolates or specialty teas.

Turn Your Story Into Cash: Writing & Launching Your Book

Worksheet

For my editor, I'll hire: _____.

My publishing coach will be: _____.

I'd like to work with _____ as my publicity manager.

My book formatter will be: _____.

If I need a virtual assistant during the launch phase, I'll reach out to: _____.

For my book cover, I really like these ideas:

1.

2.

3.

4.

5.

Publishing Your Book

I plan to self-publish on these sites:

1.

2.

3.

4.

5.

I will be offering print-on-demand from _____

for the price of _____ per book.

My book blurb needs to cover these points:

1.

2.

3.

4.

5.

This is my author bio: _____

_____

_____

_____

I will send advanced reading copies to the following people:

1.

2.

3.

4.

5.

Items I need to gather for my media kit include:

1.

2.

3.

4.

5.

Publishing Your Book

I want to offer a blog tour at these places

1.

2.

3.

4.

5.

Section 4

Marketing Your Book

Some new authors believe if you write and publish a book, hungry readers will beat down your door to buy it. Unfortunately, that's not true. Your book is competing with millions of others for the time and attention of your readers.

So, you have to become proactive about selling your book. No one will buy your book or know it exists without some hardcore marketing on your part. The good news is that there are plenty of different promotional tactics you can use to build your reader base.

Advertise Your Book on Social Media

One of the best ways to get some traffic to your book and find new readers is to use social media advertising. If you're not familiar with the concept, you pay a social media network of your choice to display an advertisement to other users.

Some authors sign up for social media advertising before they truly understand how to get the best results. It's not about how many people see your ad. It's about how many people in your target market see your advertisement.

For example, it's better to have an advertisement that's seen by twenty thousand fantasy readers than an advertisement seen by two million readers who don't enjoy that genre. That's because the fantasy readers are more likely to sign up for your mailing list or buy your book than the other readers.

To learn more about your audience, look at your statistics about them. On Facebook and Instagram, these statistics are called Insights. Pinterest and Twitter call this data 'analytics'. Regardless of the name, you need to

Marketing Your Book

regularly examine this data and mine it for information you can use to connect with your readers.

You might discover things about your target market that you hadn't anticipated. You might expect that teens are most likely to buy your young adult book. But your statistics show that it's not just teens buying your books. Older adults enjoy the genre, too. This means when it's time to create social advertisements, you don't want to limit it to a certain age group.

Using social media sites like Facebook, Twitter, Pinterest or Instagram can be helpful to fiction writers. If you're a non-fiction author and your book is about business or leadership topics, you'll probably see better results when you use LinkedIn to advertise your book. That's because your target market is primarily business professionals.

Don't think you have to take out a huge ad and spends thousands on your first social media advertisement. It's smart to start by running a few small ads first. This prevents you from wasting money on an ineffective ad and it shows you what your audience best responds to.

Another advantage of starting with small ads is that you can measure your return on investment, so you can learn what to expect from your campaigns. For example, you may find that campaigns that run on Wednesday perform better than ads that run over the weekend. This is valuable data, so make sure you're tracking your results.

Whether you're launching a huge advertisement or a tiny one, make sure the ad displays nicely on mobile devices like smart phones and tablets. A smaller device may make your text difficult to read or cut your picture size in half. If you forget to test the ad, it may flop and you'll be left wondering what happened.

Don't forget that you aren't limited to text and images for your advertisement. You can create video ads that showcase your book and encourage users to buy it. Keep your video short and focused, as most social users won't stick around to watch long videos. Good video ideas could include: a professionally designed book trailer, a quick tutorial related to your niche, a brief Q & A session, or a short behind the scenes segment explaining your inspiration for the book.

Social media advertising really does work. It can take a few weeks to figure out how to get the best results, so don't give up too soon. Instead, keep setting up ads and tweaking them as you learn more about your reader base.

How to Advertise Your Book on Reading Websites

Social media advertising is one way to get the word out about your book. There are also a variety of reading websites and blogs where you can advertise your book. The advantage of using a reading website is the visitors are readers by nature. So, you're more likely to convert a browser into a buyer simply by showcasing your book.

Advertising on a book site also gives your book more visibility. On a large social media site, your advertisement will compete with millions of other ads. With a reading site, the competition isn't as fierce, meaning your book will have the chance to stand out.

If you're ready to start advertising on reading sites, the first thing you need to do is make a list of sites where you could advertise. Here are a few you may want to consider:
- Book Bub
- The eReader Café
- Just Kindle Books
- Booktastik
- Riffle Select
- Kindle Nation Daily
- The Fussy Librarian
- Robin Reads

After you have a big list of reading websites, start reviewing them to see if they're right for your book. Some reading sites will only promote certain types of books. For example, Kindle Nation Daily only supports Kindle books. If you didn't choose to make your book available through Kindle, then KND isn't the right platform for you.

Another thing to consider as you're reviewing sites is if your genre is popular with that audience. For example, Just Kindle Books shares this: "Our top performing genres are romance, mystery/thriller, erotic romance, paranormal fiction, women's fiction, cooking and self-help."

This means your funny middle grade novel probably won't get a lot of traction on JKB and submitting an advertisement would waste your time and the time of the editors behind the site. Instead, make a note that this website isn't a good fit and keep looking.

Once you've finished, you should have a list of reading sites where your book would fit best. Now it's time to start submitting your advertisement. Most sites have strict guidelines about what they won't accept. Don't just blindly ignore these guidelines.

The guidelines are there for a purpose. The readers of these sites expect certain things (maybe a set price point or certain cover size) and the website owner wants to keep her readers happy. If you show disregard for her community, she's not likely to support your book no matter how much you're willing to pay.

After you've read and followed the guidelines, submit your book and any accompanying information like your genre or page count. Most site owners will have a form you can fill out or will ask you to send them an email.

If your book sounds like a good fit, the site owner or content editor will follow up with you. She'll explain how her process works and collect payment from you. If you have any questions about how your book will be promoted, now is the time to ask.

Keep in mind that as you release more books, you may be interacting with this site owner again in the future. So, be sure to pay promptly and stay professional in your messages.

Using Giveaways to Promote Your Book

A great way to promote your recently published book is to use giveaways. You offer participants the chance to win something and in exchange they perform a certain action, like subscribing to your newsletter. The advantage of a giveaway is it attracts lots of attention and can really help you grow your platform, if done right. Before you schedule your first content, here's what you need to keep in mind:

Have a Goal

Be honest about what you want from your giveaway contest. Are you looking to gain more newsletter subscribers? Do you want to gain another 500 likes to your Facebook fan page? Are you hoping for a fresh round of reviews on Amazon?

Turn Your Story Into Cash: Writing & Launching Your Book

Once you know what you want, you can plan your contest around this outcome. For example, if you want 200 more newsletter subscribers, then one of your contest requirements might be joining your mailing list.

Follow the Rules

Each social media platform has special rules for running contests. Facebook doesn't allow you to make liking your Facebook fan page a requirement for entry. They do this because they don't want people inflating their page with fans that really don't care and are only there for the prize.

However, you can ask your contest participants to like your Facebook page. You can't use it as a requirement. You also need to clarify that Facebook isn't endorsing or supporting your contest.

Set a Deadline

A contest needs a quick deadline to motivate people to take action. Otherwise, participants decide they'll enter later and they never quite get around to it. That's why you want to run your contest for about a week. Anything longer and you may see a loss of interest.

Choose Your Prizes

It's tempting to give away your book as a prize, but don't do this. Your goal is to sell books. When participants think they have a chance to win your book, they don't buy it. Instead, they enter your contest and hope they're the winner.

However, there are plenty of other items you could giveaway as prizes. You could create promo swag using a site like Zazzle. Using Zazzle, you can create branded journals, pens, canvas totes, mugs, and more.

You're not limited to print on demand items. You can also choose prizes that relate to the theme of your book. For example, if your book is about royalty in the medieval ages, then a prize could be a small tiara or crown.

If your book is non-fiction, then you may want to offer a service or another product as a giveaway. As a niche leader, you may decide the prize is a one-hour consultation with you or it could be an exclusive code to your insider's club.

Don't throw together a giveaway randomly. Take some time to think through what the rules will be, what prize you'll offer, and how participants can enter to win. Your contest will flow smoothly if you work these details out in advance.

Polishing Your Author Page

Many publishing platforms allow you to create an author page on their website. This page is where readers can go to learn more about you and your other books. It's a smart marketing move to have your author page completely filled out and polished. It makes readers, other authors, and industry professionals think you're a knowledgeable leader in your niche.

There are a few key things you want to make sure you have on your author page. The first is reviews or endorsements from other people. If a book reviewer called the voice of your book melodious then use that quote. If a fellow author endorsed your book and said it was an intriguing tale, be sure to put that up.

These reviews are social proof that makes readers more willing to take a chance on your book. But what if you don't have reviews yet? What if you're still trying to get your book noticed? Then it's time to start asking for what you want.

Don't be afraid to approach a few book bloggers and ask them for their honest thoughts. If you have author friends, reach out and explain that you're looking for an endorsement. Most reviewers and fellow authors will help you out if you only ask.

After you've added some endorsements, update your biography. Keep it short and highlight any special qualifications you have that might relate to your writing. If you write medical thrillers and you were a nurse for 25 years, then mention that in your bio. It adds credibility to your author brand.

Now, you need to include a picture of yourself. This should be a smiling head shot of you in good lighting. It can be tempting to use that picture from twenty years ago when you were young and skinny.

A big part of building your author brand is making sure you're recognizable today. That means your photo should be a recent one, preferably taken some time in the last two to three years. Remember, this is a photo that will follow you around the internet. So, pick a shot that makes you feel confident and beautiful.

Next, it's time to work on your links. Some platforms allow you to link to your website, blog, and all of your social media sites. If your platform only allows you to publish one link, then that link should be to your website so you can drive traffic to it.

Amazon's author pages allow you to include videos. If you have a professionally made book trailer, then you'll want to make sure you submit that video to your profile. You may also want to add a video introduction so readers can get to know you and get a feel for your personality. Aim to keep it short, think under three minutes, and remember to smile while you talk. It makes you look friendly and approachable.

Don't just abandon your author profiles. Keep them updated every six months and if new author features are added, be sure to try them out. This helps expand the reach of your author brand.

Creating & Building Your Email List

Imagine releasing your next book and being able to tell thousands of readers who love your work about it. Imagine being able to contact these readers anytime you want with news or updates about your books. With your own mailing list, this isn't just a dream. It's entirely possible.

The first thing you need to do to build your email list is choose a mailing list service. There are a few really good options including Constant Contact, Aweber, and Get Response.

Mailing list services charge you by the number of subscribers you have. For a list of 500 subscribers, you can expect to pay $15-25 per month. As your list grows and you get more subscribers, you'll get charged more. However, if you're regularly marketing to your list, then you should easily be able to cover this cost.

If your budget is tight, look into MailChimp. They allow their users to have a free mailing list if they have less than 2,000 subscribers. That means you can build your list for free. Once you have more than two thousand subscribers, you'll have to pay a monthly fee.

Marketing Your Book

Now that you've done some research and picked a mailing list company, it's time to get started building your list. Your service provider will give you a special code you can use on your website to add a subscription form.

If you're not familiar with HTML or other coding languages, ask your web designer to put it on your blog for you. Ideally, you need to have your subscription form on the right side of your blog and you need to have it underneath your posts. This makes it easy for your visitors to sign up for your mailing list.

It's smart to offer a free gift to encourage new visitors to sign up for your list. This free gift could be a collection of short stories, bonus content from you, or a free book of yours.

Be sure the free gift matches your other work. If you write sweet romance, then offering a horror book will seem a bit odd and won't help build your platform. Instead, offer a short sweet romance to your visitors and you'll see better results.

Now that you have a mailing list and special offer in place, it's time to let the world know. Share about your special gift on social media and invite your followers to sign up for your mailing list. You should also put a link to your mailing list at the back of all of your published books.

Don't forget to create a special landing page on your website. This page should mention your free gift and invite visitors to enter their contact information. Once visitors do this, they should immediately be directed to a 'thank you' page.

Now, if you're featured on a webinar or podcast episode, you can tell listeners to head to a specific page on your website in order to sign up for your mailing list. This can convert more visitors to subscribers, because you're only asking them to do one thing (sign up for your list).

Building an email list of readers who love your books is one of the best ways to grow your career as an author. Experiment with different free gifts to see which one appeals the most to your audience.

Interacting in Groups & Forums

One simple way to market your book is to interact in groups and forums. This can help drive traffic to your website and boost the visibility of your

Turn Your Story Into Cash: Writing & Launching Your Book

work. You don't want to pick just any group or forum to participate in. You want to choose ones that will help you grow your brand.

For non-fiction authors, this means you should pick groups that are in your niche. For example, if your book is about dog care, then joining a forum focused on dog training or dog health would be a good idea. This will give you a chance to answer questions and establish yourself as an authority on the topic.

For fiction authors, this means you need to join groups built around your genre. For example, if you write fantasy and paranormal books, you should look for groups created specifically for fantasy readers.

Participating regularly in groups will also give you lots of content ideas. This means you'll have plenty of inspiration to record Facebook Live videos and make blog posts. But the inspiration doesn't stop there. The more you learn about your audience, the easier it will be to target them with your subsequent books.

Along with groups where your readers hang out, you also want to join groups where you can find fellow authors. If you write romance, then look for groups that focus on romance writing. Pick places where the mood is upbeat and authors encourage each other. If you join a group that's negative or thrives on picking people apart, you'll be pulled down by all the negativity.

When you are part of a group, remember to engage in discussions. It can be tempting to parrot what everyone else is saying. You want to focus on adding value to each conversation. If you regularly share helpful information and encourage other members, you'll develop a reputation as a trusted leader in your niche.

If forum or group etiquette allows self-promotion, share about your books when joining in conversations. The key here is to only do this when your book is relevant to the topic at hand. If someone asks how you know if your dog is sick, then it could be appropriate to link to your book on dog healthcare. It wouldn't be appropriate to link to your book about computer programming.

If you're not sure about the rules of etiquette in the group or forum, take a moment to reach out to the owner or a moderator. This shows you're there because you genuinely care and want to help better this online community.

Position Yourself as an Expert

You want to become the go-to source for advice in your community. That means stepping up and positioning yourself as an expert. Being an expert doesn't mean you have all the answers or that you develop a big ego. Being an expert means you're a leader who cares about and protects your community. So, how can you be seen as an expert? Try doing some of these things:

Get Featured on Podcasts

Find podcasts in your niche and start listening. Which ones do you enjoy the most? Which hosts sound like they'd be a good fit for your personality? If you find several possibilities, write them down so you know who you need to contact.

After you've found a few podcasts, pop onto their websites. Check to see if the host is looking for more guests. If you can't find any information about being a guest speaker, reach out to the host directly. Ask her what her criteria is for choosing guests and see if you fit the bill.

Build Your Own Group

Leading a group is a great way to show that you're an expert in your niche. But you should only start a group if you're willing to invest time and attention into growing it. At first, you'll spend most of your time marketing the group (about 5-10 hours a week).

As the group grows in numbers, you'll start getting members who heard about you through word of mouth and want to join in the fun. Pay attention to who is joining your group and remove anyone that attempts to spam your tribe or starts flame wars. These are not the type of people you want to be associated with personally or professionally.

Find Journalist Requests

There are websites where journalists will post about what stories they're working on and request experts to interview. This can be an excellent way to boost your visibility and be seen as a thought leader.

Some of these sites, like Help A Reporter Out, are free to join. If you want additional features, you may want to purchase a monthly subscription. The reporter's requests are sorted according to niche, making it easy for you to scan for opportunities that are right for you.

When you first start promoting yourself as an expert, you may not get a lot of traction. Keep sharing your knowledge and doors will begin to open for you.

Promoting Your Book Offline

Even if your book is digital only, there are still plenty of ways you can promote offline. All it takes is a little bit of planning and persistence.

Give Branded Gifts to Strangers

You can start by carrying promotional gifts with you. These don't have to be huge items. They can be pens, notepads, or coffee mugs with your website address and author tagline. You can pass these items out as you meet people. Give a cashier your bookmark or hand a pen to the lady in line behind you at the bank.

Attend Conferences

Grow your reader base by attending conferences in your niche. This will help you form valuable industry relationships, too. Don't try to meet and interact with every single person attending.

Instead, focus on serving others and making genuine connections with a few people. If someone asks what you do, be prepared with a short pitch about your book. If you have bookmarks or other promotional items with your cover on it, you can pass them out.

Speak at Events

Look around for seminars and networking events that could use a speaker. If you know the event budget is tiny and you want the experience of speaking, offer to do the job for free. You can also ask if the event coordinator is agreeable to you making a two minute pitch about your book at the end of your presentation.

If possible, have someone there to record your speech so you can upload it to a video site. This will not only show off your speaking abilities, it

Marketing Your Book

also gives you a chance to turn your offline content into an online marketing opportunity.

Not comfortable speaking to groups? Try joining an organization like Toastmasters. Local groups meet monthly so members can improve their speaking skills. If you'd like to speak at events regularly, this can be a great way to jump start your speaking career.

Don't be afraid to talk about your book or promote it to others. Most people look at writers and authors a bit like celebrities. They're fascinated by what you do and curious to know more.

Marketing your book can be fun and rewarding. The more you do it, the easier it gets. Remember to take notes about what's working for you and what isn't. This will help you have plenty of promotion ideas when it's time to launch your next book!

Checklist

Marketing your book can be a thrilling adventure. It's all about getting the word out about your book so the right readers can find it. If you're stumped on how to market and advertise your book, try doing some of these activities:

Advertising Your Book on Social Media

- [ ] Use analytics and insights. Many social media platforms have data about your followers and fans that you can dig into. Take the time to learn more about your audience so you can tailor your ads.
- [ ] Start with small ads. Don't waste money on huge ads if you've never advertised before. Instead, focus on trying a few small ads to see how your community responds.
- [ ] Get your ads to display on mobile. Social media users love browsing social sites on their smart phones and tablets. This means all of your ads need to be mobile optimized to get the best results from your ads.
- [ ] Track the results of your ads. The more you track your data, the better your advertising campaigns will become.
- [ ] Include videos as part of your advertising strategy. Consumers love videos, so don't be afraid to experiment with book trailers, behind the scenes features, and even bonus content videos.

Advertising Your Book on Reading Websites

- [ ] Make a list of reading websites. Look for bloggers and site owners that are getting a lot of traffic and interaction from their fans.
- [ ] Check to see if they promote your genre. If a blogger doesn't promote your genre, then don't waste your time trying to advertise with them. You probably won't see a good return on that investment.
- [ ] Look for guidelines. Most book blogs have guidelines that explain how they prefer to work with authors. They may also have special requirements that you need to meet in order to be featured on the website.
- [ ] Submit your listing. Once you've read through the guidelines, submit your listing to the site owner. If she's interested, you should hear back within 2-3 weeks.

Using Giveaways to Promote Your Book

- [ ] Have a goal. Before you create a contest, think about what you want that contest to achieve. Are you looking to get more visibility for your book? Promote your upcoming series?
- [ ] Follow the rules. If you'll be using social media as part of your contest, take time to check that platform's guidelines. There may be some restrictions that you need to be aware of.
- [ ] Set a deadline. Don't drag out your contest or followers will lose interest. Instead, focus on a tight time line of 7-14 days.
- [ ] Choose your prizes. Before you announce your contest, pick prizes and think about how you'll declare a winner. Will it be done randomly? Will it be a 'best of...' award? These are important bits of information you need to include in your contest rules.

Polishing Your Author Page

- [ ] Post endorsements. If authors or bloggers have endorsed you or said lovely things about your writing, you can add these reviews to your author profile.
- [ ] Update your biography. Include details from your life that are relevant and will help grow your author brand. For example, if your book is on dog care and you're a veterinarian, mention this fact in your bio.
- [ ] Upload a recent head shot. Readers want to get to know the person behind their favorite books. That means uploading a head shot of your smiling face.
- [ ] Link to your website. Make sure that visitors to your author profile can quickly find your website so they can sign up for your mailing list.
- [ ] Add your book trailer. Amazon allows authors to add their book trailers if they wish.

Creating and Building Your Email List

- [ ] Choose a mailing list company. Pick a service that you like and find easy to use. You'll most likely need them for years to come, so make sure you're happy with your choice.
- [ ] Add an email form to your website. If you have a web designer, send him or her the code and they'll upload it to your website for you.
- [ ] Offer a free gift. This is a great way to get more people to sign up for your author newsletter. Just make sure your free gift is relevant to your audience.

- [ ] Create a special landing page. Once you have a gift available, make a landing page on your website that invites visitors to join your newsletter. If you don't know how to make a landing page, ask your web designer.
- [ ] Make a thank you page. After someone signs up for your list, have a page on your website that thanks them and gives them the chance to follow you on social media.

Interacting in Groups and Forums

- [ ] Find groups in your niche. If you're not sure where to start with your search, look for Facebook and LinkedIn groups that appeal to you.
- [ ] Offer helpful advice. When there are discussions in the group, share your thoughts. Try to interact in the discussions 2-3 times a week so you become a regular.
- [ ] Stay positive and kind. Nothing will kill your career faster than going onto niche groups and acting like a jerk. Even if someone else is unkind to you, don't be unkind to them.
- [ ] Ask before linking to your book. Group creators are often protective of their communities because they don't want them spammed. For this reason, you should always ask the site owner before you link to your books or your website.

Position Yourself as an Expert

- [ ] Get featured on podcasts. Look around for podcasts you enjoy, and then reach out to the host to see if you'd be a good fit for a guest spot.
- [ ] Start your own group. Create a group for those in your niche using Facebook groups or LinkedIn groups. This gives you the chance to show off your expertise to group members.
- [ ] Become a source for journalists. There are a variety of sites that allow you to connect with reporters around the world. If a journalist likes what you said, she may quote you in a national publication, boosting the visibility of both you and your book.

Promoting Your Book Offline

- [ ] Hand out branded gifts. Use a service like Zazzle to create merchandise and small gifts that are branded with your website or book title. This gives you a natural way to work what you do into conversations.
- [ ] Attend conferences in your niche. Focus on serving others and connecting with them. Building genuine relationships with people in your niche

Marketing Your Book

is one of the best ways to grow your career.
- ☐ Speak at events. Start small and local. If you find you enjoy speaking, then begin pitching event coordinators and letting them know how you can be of service.
- ☐ Join Toastmasters or another speaking club. Become part of an organization that helps you refine your speaking skills. This can lead to even more promotional opportunities later down the road.

Turn Your Story Into Cash: Writing & Launching Your Book

Worksheet

My book will be published on: _____.

I'll share my book release on these social media platforms:
_____.

To celebrate my launch, I'll do these promotional activities:

1.

2.

3.

4.

5.

I'll reach out to these people for endorsements:

1.

2.

3.

4.

5.

Marketing Your Book

I'll be advertising on these reading websites:

1.

2.

3.

4.

5.

My mailing list provider is: _____.

My login details are: _____

The free gift opt-in for the newsletter list will be: _____.

To set up my newsletter, I'll ask for help from: _____.

For my book promotion giveaways, my goal is to _____.

The give-away participation rules will be

1.

2.

3.

Turn Your Story Into Cash: Writing & Launching Your Book

The deadline for participation is: _____

Prizes I plan to hand out include:

1.

2.

3.

4.

5.

To help position myself as an expert, I will be participating in the following groups or communities:

1.

2.

3.

4.

5.

I'll also be: _____

_____

_____

Order Form

Email orders: judi@judimoreo.com

Telephone orders: +1-702-283-4567
Please have your credit card ready.

Postal orders: Turning Point International
3315 E. Russell Road, Ste. A4-404
Las Vegas, Nevada 89120
USA

See our website www.judimoreo.com for FREE information on: Other books, *Choices* magazine, Speaking/Seminars, Consulting

Name: _____

Address: _____

City: _____

State/Province: _____ Postal Code: _____

Telephone: _____

Email: _____

Amount: _____

Sales Tax: _____

Shipping by air: _____

Payment Type: ☐ Check ☐ Credit Card (Visa, MasterCard, AMEX)

Card Number: _____

Name on Card: _____

Expiration Date: _____ / _____ Billing Zip Code: _____

www.ingramcontent.com/pod-product-compliance
Lightning Source LLC
Chambersburg PA
CBHW050605300426
44112CB00013B/2078